A Lenten Journey Towards Christian Maturity

A Daily Prayer Guide

By

Father William E. Breslin

God bless Kay Lorenz

Father Bill Breslin

2/22/09

100 Talents Press

Published by 100 Talents Press, an imprint of Pearn and
Associates, Inc., Boulder, Colorado. For general information
about other products and services, please contact us at
happypoet@hotmail.com (720) 406-8858.

Cover design by Anne Kilgore.

Library of Congress Control Number: 2008932516

Breslin, William, E., 1948
A Lenten Journey Towards Christian Maturity,
by Father William E. Breslin, first edition.
ISBN 978-0-9777318-4-8 paperback

For my high school principal
Sister Mary, RSM
who taught thousands to
"Dare to be different"

Contents

Ash Wednesday *3*

    Thursday after Ash Wednesday *6*

    Friday after Ash Wednesday *9*

    Saturday after Ash Wednesday *12*

The First Sunday of Lent *15*

    Monday of the First Week of Lent *18*

    Tuesday of the First Week of Lent *21*

    Wednesday of the First Week of Lent *24*

    Thursday of the First Week of Lent *27*

    Friday of the First Week of Lent *30*

    Saturday of the First Week of Lent *33*

The Second Sunday of Lent *36*

    Monday of the Second Week of Lent *39*

    Tuesday of the Second Week of Lent *42*

    Wednesday of the Second Week of Lent *45*

    Thursday of the Second Week of Lent *48*

    Friday of the Second Week of Lent *51*

    Saturday of the Second Week of Lent *54*

The Third Sunday of Lent *57*

      Monday of the Third Week of Lent *60*

      Tuesday of the Third Week of Lent *64*

      Wednesday of the Third Week of Lent *67*

      Thursday of the Third Week of Lent *70*

      Friday of the Third Week of Lent *73*

      Saturday of the Third Week of Lent *76*

The Fourth Sunday of Lent *79*

      Monday of the Fourth Week of Lent *82*

      Tuesday of the Fourth Week of Lent *85*

      Wednesday of the Fourth Week of Lent *88*

      Thursday of the Fourth Week of Lent *91*

      Friday of the Fourth Week of Lent *94*

      Saturday of the Fourth Week of Lent *97*

The Fifth Sunday of Lent *100*

      Monday of the Fifth Week of Lent *103*

      Tuesday of the Fifth Week of Lent *106*

      Wednesday of the Fifth Week of Lent *109*

      Thursday of the Fifth Week of Lent *112*

      Friday of the Fifth Week of Lent *115*

      Saturday of the Fifth Week of Lent *118*

Author Biography *121*

"Above all, our need at this moment in history is a people who, through an enlightened and lived faith, render God credible in this world."

Cardinal Joseph Ratzinger

April 1, 2005

The day before the death of Pope John Paul II.

Ash Wednesday

"I would like to show them how beautiful it is to be Christian, because the widespread idea which continues to exist is that Christianity is composed of laws and bans which one has to keep and, hence, is something toilsome and burdensome – that one is freer without such a burden."

Benedict XVI, just before World Youth Day 2005 Cologne.

Many Catholics think of their religion as a collection of many rules and obligations. Not living up to these rules and obligations leaves many feeling either that the rules and obligations are no good, or they themselves are no good.

This is like a teenager reacting to a parent's laying down the law about curfew time. Such a family rule is either to be obeyed, or ridiculed, or eluded perhaps with a white lie, depending on the attitude of the teen. Or the teen can react with anger and a verbal attack against Mom and Dad being unreasonable, out of step with the times.

Too many of us Catholics deal with our religion as if we were teenagers in rebellion, or feeling that our obligation is slavish obedience. **This is not Christian maturity.**

If this is where you are spiritually, then hear the word of the Lord:

"We have much to say about this, but it is hard to explain because you are slow to learn. In fact, though by this time you ought to be teachers, you need someone to teach you the elementary truths of God's word all over again. You need milk, not solid food! Anyone who lives on milk, being still an infant, is not acquainted with the teaching about righteousness. But solid food is for the mature, who by constant use have trained themselves to distinguish good from evil."

(Hebrews 5: 11-14)

This Lenten Daily Prayer Guide is an invitation to move through the elementary truths of our Catholic Faith into solid food fit for spiritually mature disciples of Jesus Christ. Why? So that we all may become adult, intelligent members of the Church, "who, through an enlightened and lived faith, render God credible in this world."

I ask myself: Am I a mature Catholic? Or do I find in my Church so many hot-button issues that I am either angry, or tepid, or even numb when it comes to thinking about my Catholic Faith? Or, am I defensive for the Church?

Prayer

Lord Jesus Christ, I firmly believe that *You* are truly present in the Eucharist. If it weren't for the Eucharist, how could I keep any of my faith alive in this storm tossed world and this buffeted Church of Yours? So I begin this Lenten Journey by affirming my faith that in the Eucharist *You* are truly present, Body, Blood, Soul and Divinity. *"I believe, O Lord, help my unbelief."* (Mark 9:24)

Thursday after Ash Wednesday

"According to some [currents of thought in our time], the time of certainties is irrevocably past, and the human being must now learn to live in a horizon of total absence of meaning, where everything is provisional and ephemeral."

Paragraph 91, *Fides et Ratio*, 1998
Encyclical by Pope John Paul II

Certitude, truth! We live in a time that wants to echo the cynical response of Pontius Pilate: "Truth, what is that!" That was right after Jesus, on trial, said, *"Anyone who wants to know the truth comes to me."*

(John 18: 37-38)

To appreciate the magnitude of the gift we have been given as human beings to search for truth, let's look back in time to 1700 years ago when St. Gregory of Nyssa said, "The soul shows its royal and exalted character . . . in that it is free, self-governed, and swayed autonomously by its own will. Of whom else can this be said, save a king?"

Slavish obedience to someone else's thought process is not the kind of maturity the Catholic Church is looking for from her members:

Human dignity requires one to act through conscious and free choice, as motivated and prompted personally from within, and not through blind impulse or merely external pressure. People achieve such dignity when they free themselves from all subservience to their feelings, and in a free choice of the good, pursue their own end by effectively and assiduously marshalling the appropriate means.

(Vatican II, *Gaudium et Spes* 17)

So we are inherently free to search after truth, or to avoid it, or in the minds of some today, to deny that there is any truth at all, or to say that everyone can find his or her own truth. As mature Catholics we are invited to use our freedom not for self-indulgence, but for the search for truth, beauty and goodness.

"The supreme exemplars of freedom for John Paul II are the martyrs. They are the heroic persons who are so committed to the known good that they stand up under pressures that would overcome the willpower of most others. Given the choice between denying their principles and losing their lives, they freely lay down their lives and thereby give witness to the truth. Jesus, who freely laid down his life for our sakes, sets the pattern for martyrs."

John Paul II and the Truth about Freedom,
by Cardinal Avery Dulles, 1995

I ask myself: In matters of conscience, am I more directed by my own opinions, or am I open to the possibility that there may be truth in Scripture and Church teachings?

Prayer

Lord, help me see that in a world without truth, freedom loses its foundation and we are exposed to the violence of passion and to manipulation, both open and hidden. Amen

Friday after Ash Wednesday

"The deepest poverty is the inability of joy, the tediousness of a life considered absurd and contradictory. This poverty is widespread today, in very different forms in the materially rich as well as the poor countries. The inability of joy presupposes and produces the inability to love, produces jealousy, avarice – all defects that devastate the life of individuals and of the world."

The New Evangelization,
by Joseph Cardinal Ratzinger

The real question we need to ask ourselves this Lent is the core question before all human beings: How shall we live? So this Lent, let us go on the journey of finding out the best way to live, which Jesus taught us, so that we may have *"joy that the world cannot give."*

This journey will require a "metanoia." This is the Greek word for "converting."

It means:

- to rethink – to question one's own way of living and
  our common way of living;
- to allow God to enter into the criteria of one's life;
- to not merely judge according to the current opinions.

To convert also means:

- not to live as all the others live,
- not to do what all do,
- not to feel justified in dubious, ambiguous, evil
  actions just because others do the same;
- to begin to see one's life through the eyes of God;
- to look for the good, even if uncomfortable;
- not aiming at the judgment of the majority, of men,
  but on the justice of God.

In other words: to convert means to look for a new style of life, a new life.

I ask myself: Am I willing to undergo this process called conversion?

Scripture: *"I tell you the truth: unless you change and become like little children, you will never enter the kingdom of heaven."* (Matt. 18:3)

The first change to make towards a new life is to make the leap of faith that truth can indeed be found in Jesus Christ who is *"the Way, the Truth and the Life."* Without this leap of faith, our religion will be a burden, not the path to *"the joy that the world cannot give."*

Prayer

Jesus, my God, I love You with my whole heart and above all things, because You are the one supreme Good and an infinitely perfect Being. You have given Your life for me, a poor sinner, and in Your mercy You have offered Yourself as food for my soul. My God, I love You. Inflame my heart so that I may love You more. Amen.

Saturday after Ash Wednesday

The Five Basic Truths of our Catholic Faith

"Certainly, in order to have a good conscience (1 Tim 1:5), *man must seek the truth and must make judgments in accordance with that same truth."* As the Apostle Paul says, *"the conscience must be confirmed by the Holy Spirit* (cf. Rom 9:1); *it must be clear* (2 Tim 1:3); *it must not practice cunning and tamper with God's word, but openly state the truth"* (cf. 2 Cor 4:2). On the other hand, the Apostle also warns Christians: *"Do not be conformed to this world but be transformed by the renewal of your mind, that you may prove what is the will of God, what is good and acceptable and perfect."* (Rom 12:2)

The Splendor of the Truth,
Encyclical of Pope John Paul II, Paragraph 62

If we are to be mature Christians we need to possess a "good conscience." Someone who wants a good conscience must seek the truth and not tamper with God's Word. Before we move into moral issues that involve our consciences we must openly state the truth.

There are five basic truths of our faith. If we do not take the leap of faith on these basic truths, then we cannot move towards Christian maturity.

I ask myself: What, then, are these basic truths of our Catholic Faith?

Truth I: God's Plan

• God has a plan; and that plan is that God loves us and wants us to be joyful and live life to the full.

Truth II: The Problem

• There is a problem; and the problem is sin. The result of sin is unhappiness, wide scale suffering, and the failure to know God's love.

Truth III: The Solution

• There is a solution; and the solution is Jesus Christ. Only through Him can we know God's love and find the joy filled way to live life to the full.

Truth IV: Our Response

• To experience this solution in our lives, we need to undergo a conversion of heart, make a commitment to Jesus Christ, receive His Holy Spirit, and embrace His Church.

Truth V: Our Reward

• The reward for making this response to Jesus Christ is joy. This joy is sustained by an on-going conversion, a life of compassion and service to the values of Christ and His Church. When this life is done, the reward is heaven.

Prayer

Good Jesus, in You alone I place all my hope. You are my salvation and my strength and the source of all good. Through Your mercy and through Your Passion, Death and Resurrection, I hope to obtain pardon of my sins, the grace of final perseverance and the eternal life of the world to come. Amen.

The First Sunday of Lent

The First Truth of our Faith:
God's Plan for Us Is Our Happiness.

"I know well the plans I have in mind for you, says the Lord, plans for your welfare, not for woe! Plans to give you a future full of hope." (Jer. 29:11)

This week's question: Do I really believe that God's plan for us is our happiness? How can that be when there is so much suffering, not only in the world, but in my own life?

Before we begin to investigate the believability of the first basic truth, that God's plan for us is our happiness, we must look at how we Catholics see God by way of a few Scriptures:

• Psalm 86 captures one aspect of the God we believe in: *"You, O Lord, are a kind and loving God, always patient, always kind and merciful."* (Ps. 86: 15)

• God is also *"compassion and love, slow to anger, and rich in mercy."* (Ps. 103: 8)

- But God also knows the inner thoughts of our hearts and holds us responsible for what we do with the precious gift of life: *"Indeed, the word of God is living and effective, sharper than any two-edged sword, penetrating even between soul and spirit, joints and marrow, and able to discern reflections and thoughts of the heart. No creature is concealed from him, but everything is naked and exposed to the eyes of him to whom we must render an account."* (Heb. 4:12-13)

- This loving yet just God *"shows no partiality, but in every nation anyone who fears him and does what is right is acceptable to him."* (Acts 10: 34-35)

- Therefore, faithful Catholics may not consider themselves as superior to people of other faiths, or to anyone. However, Catholics are called to realize that Jesus Christ *"is the one ordained by God to be judge of the living and the dead."* (Acts 10: 42)

So, I ask myself: Do I really believe that God wants me to be happy?

Prayer

Lord Jesus Christ, the true life, You give hope and purpose to our earthly existence. Open our minds and hearts to the goodness and beauty of the world around us, to solidarity and friendship with our fellow human beings, to intimate communion with God our Father, in a love that goes beyond all limits of time and space, to eternal, unassailable happiness. Amen.

Adapted from a talk given
by John Paul II, Denver, 1993

Monday of the First Week of Lent

The First Truth of our Faith:
God's Plan for Us Is Our Happiness.

"Those who plan what is good, find love and faithfulness." (Proverbs 14: 22)

What about all the woe and suffering?

"Considering the world of suffering in its personal and at the same time collective meaning, one cannot fail to notice the fact that this world, at some periods of time and in some eras of human existence, as it were becomes particularly concentrated. This happens, for example, in cases of natural disasters, epidemics, catastrophes, up-heavals and various social scourges: one thinks, for example, of a bad harvest and connected with it – or with various other causes – the scourge of famine. One thinks, finally, of war. I speak of this in a particular way. I speak of the last two World Wars, the second of which brought with it a much greater harvest of death and a much heavier burden of human sufferings."

Apostolic Letter, SALVIFICI DOLORIS, Feb. 1984,
by Pope John Paul II

So, with all of this suffering, how can we believe that God's plan for us is our happiness?

Ah, the perennial question of suffering! How can a good God let us suffer so?

The short answer is from the Letter to the Hebrews: *"For we do not have a high priest who is unable to sympathize with our weaknesses, but we have one who was tempted in every way, just as we are – yet without sin."* (Heb. 4: 15-16)

The temptation is grave indeed, especially in our own time, to let the mystery of suffering weaken our faith and so buy into the mindset that is so common in our day: that all is meaningless. "We are heirs to a civilization that has in fact killed God, in other words, that has caused absurdity and meaninglessness to prevail over meaning, and this gives rise to a deep protest . . . . Goodness is not only the response to evil, but it is also the response to meaninglessness." – from a Letter of Brother Roger of Taize to the Family of Paul Ricoeur the day after his death, May 2005.

I ask myself: How can I believe in the goodness and justice of God with so much woe in the world?

Prayer

Lord Jesus, do I prefer meaninglessness over making a leap of faith to believe in You, a good God, whose plan for us is our happiness? Which leap lands me in a better spot? Keep me faithful to You, despite all the questions and all the suffering. Amen.

Tuesday of the First Week of Lent

The First Truth of our Faith:
God's Plan for Us Is Our Happiness.

"He is the Rock, his works are perfect, and all his ways just. A faithful God who does no wrong, upright and just is he." (Deuteronomy 32: 4)

Making a leap of faith to believe in the goodness and justice of God despite all evidence to the contrary is the necessary step to move into Christian maturity.

"If we believe, then everything is illuminated and takes shape around us: chance is seen to be order, success assumes an incorruptible plenitude, suffering becomes a visit and a caress of God. But if we hesitate, the rock remains dry, the sky dark, the waters treacherous and shifting. And we may hear the voice of the Master, faced with our bungled lives: 'O men of little faith, why have you doubted . . . .'"

From Pierre Teilhard de Chardin,
The Divine Milieu (1960), p. 136

Søren Kierkegaard was a Danish philosopher in the 1800's. He was also a religious thinker who set the stage for modern existentialism and modern psychology. In his 1844 book, The Concept of Anxiety, he considered Adam's original sin and describes anxiety as a stage that is necessary before one makes the leap of faith into Christianity. Before one makes this leap of faith one comes to a point where one shudders at one's freedom. This anxiety, which perfectly describes the time in which we live, can lead to sin. (Sin will be next week's issue). Sin compounds the anxiety of freedom, and freedom is lost through sin. This cycle of sinfulness and anxiety can be broken, according to Kierkegaard, only by a leap of faith.

"Believing is possible only by grace and the interior helps of the Holy Spirit. But it is no less true that believing is an authentically human act. Trusting in God and cleaving to the truths he has revealed are contrary neither to human freedom nor to human reason. Even in human relations it is not contrary to our dignity to believe what other persons tell us about themselves and their intentions or to trust their promises (for example, when a man and a woman marry) to share a communion of life with one another."

Catechism of the Catholic Church, Paragraph 154

I ask myself: Am I willing to make this initial step: to make an act of faith that God exists and that God is good?

Prayer

Dear Lord, the Great Healer, I kneel before you, since every perfect gift must come from You. I pray, give skill to my hands, clear vision to my mind, kindness and meekness to my heart. Give me singleness of purpose, strength to lift up a part of the burden of my suffering fellow men, and a true realization of the privilege that is mine. Take from my heart all guile and worldliness, that with the simple faith of a child, I may rely on You.

From *A Simple Heart*, by Mother Teresa,
Published by Ballantine Books, 1995.

Wednesday of the First Week of Lent

The First Truth of our Faith:
God's Plan for Us Is Our Happiness.

"Do not conform any longer to the pattern of this world, but be transformed by the renewal of your mind."

(Romans 12:2)

Cheap Grace or Costly Grace?

Dietrich Bonhoeffer was a Lutheran pastor in Nazi Germany who wrote a book called *The Cost of Discipleship.* What he had seen was how easily his own countrymen, all of whom were Christian, had gone along with the Nazi horrors. He described this apparent Christian as wanting "cheap grace," not the "costly grace" of true discipleship.

"He wants to follow, but feels obliged to insist on his own terms to the level of human understanding. The disciple places himself at the Master's disposal, but at the same time retains the right to dictate his own terms. But then discipleship is no longer discipleship, but a program of our own to be arranged to suit ourselves, and to be judged in accordance with the standards of rational ethic."

Dietrich Bonhoeffer, *The Cost of Discipleship,* p. 66

Today we are often surrounded by nominal "Christians" who neither know God nor desire to follow Him. Bonhoeffer was surrounded by lukewarm pastors and cultural "Christians" who supported Hitler. To most of his contemporaries security and wealth had become more important than fidelity to God. Though Bonhoeffer belonged to a community of committed disciples, the larger circle of his acquaintances at work and in the larger community did not share his convictions.

Eventually he was imprisoned and separated from those who, like him, trusted in God completely.

In his hearing before the Gestapo during his imprisonment, he defied the Gestapo by openly assert-ing that, as a Christian, he was an implacable enemy of the Nazis and their totalitarian demands. He remained steadfast even though he was continually threatened with torture and, if he did not recant, with the arrest of his parents, his sisters and his fiancée. In 1944, when friends made an attempt to liberate him and to take him to safety abroad, he decided to remain in prison in order not to endanger others. Bonhoeffer was hanged by the Gestapo in 1945. He died calmly and with dignity. His life and his death were great testimony of his teaching about "costly grace."

I ask myself: Am I willing to make this leap of faith, to believe in a good God, even if it costs me dearly?

Prayer

Lord, do not let me be conformed to this world, but rather be transformed by the renewal of my mind, so that I may make this leap of faith to believe in Your goodness despite all evidence to the contrary. And, Lord, grant that I may accept the cost of this leap of faith, whatever You ask of me. I only ask that my act of faith may bring me ever closer to You. Amen.

Thursday of the First Week of Lent

The First Truth of our Faith:
God's Plan for Us Is Our Happiness.

"How can this be," Mary asked the angel, "since I know not man?" (Luke 1:34)

Does making a leap of faith mean not questioning our faith?

No.

There are some people who have the simple faith of a child, even though they have matured, through much suffering, into a ripe old age. Who of us has not been inspired by a faith-filled grandparent who might never have had a college education, but whom God tested through very great suffering? Do we not all know some such faithful Catholic who may have had to face the death of a child or a maiming car accident or a tragic death of a spouse, among many other sorrows? How did our ancestors hold on to their faith? Surely they were tempted to doubt the goodness of God, and even the existence of God. Yet our lives have been sprinkled and marked by such witnesses of faith who loved God, even in the darkness, and held firm. Such family "saints" may never have been able to offer a reasoned case for why their faith was deep. Theirs was a faith that was simply tested, and wise, but never articulated in a verbal, cognitive way.

It's quite another thing for intellectually talented and well-educated minds to practice an unquestioned faith. That could be a misuse of God's gift of our intellect, and might even be a case of intellectual sloth, or a lack of honesty or courage or depth. Unquestioned faith is not what is asked of us as adult Catholics. Remember that God who made the sun and the moon and all the galaxies of stars also made the brains of every human being. God wants us to think, and question, and grow through our doubts and struggles. And working through our questions and our doubts, we will wind up, by the grace of God, with the same tested, wise faith of our ancestors.

After all, history's greatest skeptic was not an atheist, but St. Thomas, the Apostle: *"Unless I see the nail marks in his hands and put my finger where the nails were, and put my hand into his side, I will not believe it."* (John 20: 25)

Questioning, even doubting, is not necessarily a lack of faith but rather could very well be a manifestation of faith! Sometimes questioning, even doubting, is really an insistence that God be taken seriously. It is right and good to insist that our faith be placed in, and sustained by, something other than a departure from human reasoning.

I ask myself: Am I still willing to make this leap of faith, to believe in a good God, even if it requires of me doubts and questions and the serious task of sincere inquiry?

Prayer

Lord, as our world slips into a practical atheism, a leaving of You aside as somehow irrelevant, as outside of our day to day lives, help me make the leap of faith to believe in You and in Your goodness and in your active love for me and all the world's children. As a mature thinking adult, help me to choose a mature faith in You. Help me become convinced of Your existence and Your power and Your love. Amen

Friday of the First Week of Lent

The First Truth of our Faith:
God's Plan for Us Is Our Happiness.

"I hope readers will come away caring passionately about this character, Jesus Christ, and wanting to know infinitely more about Him . . . . We have to become saints. We have to become like Christ. Anything less is simply not enough. The world doesn't need any more mediocrity or hedged bets."

Interview with Anne Rice, author of *Christ the Lord*,
in the *Borzoi Reader*

A Lenten Friday's Formal Act of Faith

On this Lenten Friday let us make a formal act of faith in God. Let us face the reality that many people in our lives have pushed God aside. Some are outright hostile to God; others are halfhearted in their response to God; and yet others are determined to write their own rules and pick and choose elements of our Catholic faith, really making up their own religion. Still others have been tormented by life's sufferings that they are no longer interested in living up to their Catholic faith.

"At first, when God is left out of the picture, everything apparently goes on as before. Mature decisions and the basic structures of life remain in place, even though they have lost their foundations. But, as Nietzsche describes it, once the news really reaches people that 'God is dead,' and they take it to heart, then everything changes."

Introduction to Christianity: Yesterday, Today, and Tomorrow, by Joseph Cardinal Ratzinger

I ask myself: Haven't we all, to a greater or lesser extent acquiesced – without being aware of it – in this wide-spread attitude: that faith in God is something subjective, that it belongs in the private realm and not in the common activities of public life? Have we not bought into an attitude that, in order to be able to get along, we all have to act now "as if there were no God"?

"I know your deeds, that you are neither hot nor cold. I wish you were either one or the other. So, because

you are lukewarm - neither hot nor cold – I am about to spit you out of my mouth." (Rev. 3:15-16)

Prayer: A Formal Act of Faith

O Lord Jesus, Savior of the World, just as the Magi brought you gifts of gold, frankincense and myrrh after a very long journey, so receive this act of faith as the culmination of my long journey to You. Let this, my act of faith in You, blossom into a love which acknowledges You, Jesus, born of Mary, as the Son of God made man. Grant me a deep friendship with You, O Christ, and lead me to be faithful and obedient to Your will. Receive, O Christ Jesus, my gifts I now freely give You: the gold of my freedom, the incense of my ardent prayer, the myrrh of my most profound affection. Amen.

Adapted from Pope Benedict XVI's
Address to Seminarians,
WYD 2005, August 19, 2005

Saturday of the First Week of Lent

Transition from God's Plan to the Problem Humanity Faces

"Enter by the narrow gate, since the road to destruction is wide and spacious, and many take it; but it is a narrow gate and a hard road that leads to life, and only a few find it." (Matt. 7:13)

Question: Since we have just affirmed our belief in God and that God is a good God who wants our happiness, there is a problem: Happiness is fleeting. Why? What is the problem with God's plan?

The problem is sin.

Question: What is sin? Sin is our making poor choices. Sin is making a choice against God and God's ways.

Question: Why do people choose sin over and against God and God's ways? People choose a way other than God's way because it is easy (at first) and because God's ways require more self-discipline.

Question: Why does God let us choose sin? God allows us to choose sin because He gave us free will. *"As for you brothers and sisters, you were called to be free. But do not let this freedom become an excuse for letting your physical desires control you."* (Gal. 5:13)

Question: It seems that we cannot exercise the self discipline we might like to. What is the problem? Our destructive tendencies are the problem and are the result of original sin.

Question: What are these "destructive tendencies" in us? Our human nature was weakened by original sin and weakened in the direction of choosing self over (and against) choosing God and His ways.

I ask myself: Can there be anything more destructive than fighting God and God's ways? *"For the flesh has desires against the Spirit, and the Spirit against the flesh; these are opposed to each other, so that you may not do what you want."* (Gal. 5:17)

Prayer

Lord Jesus Christ, as we prepare to enter the Second Week of Lent, strengthen us to look seriously at the problem of evil. Give us the boldness to call it what it is. Give us the courage to see it in our lives. And give us to honesty to not sidestep its reality in our lives. And then, Lord, show us what to do about it. Amen.

The Second Sunday of Lent

The Problem Humanity Faces: Evil

"The Lord said to Cain, 'Why are you angry? Why is your face downcast? If you do what is right, will you not be accepted? But if you do not do what is right, sin is crouching at your door; it desires to have you, but you must master it.'" (Gen. 4:6-7)

The problem of evil is the problem we all face, ever since our first parents. Yet, original sin, and sin itself, seem to be topics to be avoided. We prefer to lay blame at someone else's doorstep for the causes of our lack of joy.

What, then, is original sin?

Original sin is the condition we are all born into, the condition of having a tendency to make choices against God and God's ways, choices that destroy our joy.

We can say that a human action – i.e., a free, intelligible action, whether good or bad – is the adoption by choice of some intelligible proposal and the execution of this choice through some exterior performance. But the core of the action is the free, self-determining choice that abides in the person, making him or her to be the kind of person he or she is.

> William E. May, Michael J. McGivney,
> Professors of Moral Theology,
> John Paul II Institute for Studies on Marriage and
> Family at the Catholic University of America

However God went about creating human beings, the first ones were given a soul and a freely given relationship with God that we call "grace." Grace could only have been a freely offered gift of love; and it had to be freely accepted. When God conceived of human's freedom as the essence of what it means to be human, there is no way for human beings to be free without the possibility of the abuse of that freedom. The first humans could reject their fundamental role in the choosing of good, and they did. The result was catastrophic.

I ask myself: Have I ever noticed that a decision to do wrong disturbed my happiness?

The Catholic Church teaches that the cause of our destructive tendencies comes from "original sin," the sin of Adam and Eve. All in the animal kingdom are inclined to choose self over others. For human beings this is the first sin: to choose, with human reflection, self over and against God and God's ways. We are far more than animals.

Prayer

"Blessed is he whose transgression is forgiven, whose sins are covered. Blessed is the man whose sin the Lord does not count against him and in whose spirit is no deceit." (Psalm 32: 1-2)

Monday of the Second Week of Lent

The Problem of Evil

"The inability to understand 'original sin' and to make it understandable is really one of the most difficult problems of present-day theology and pastoral ministry."

Joseph Cardinal Ratzinger, 1985

If we do not honestly face the reality of sin and our participation in evil we will never understand the solution to this problem of evil. The solution, of course, is Jesus Christ. But if we do not realize our participation in evil, and indeed its magnetic pull on us, then we will not understand how our own evils make us enemies of God. Unless we see this enmity with God clearly, we will probably not come to understand how Jesus is our Savior.

"Do you not know that to be a lover of the world means enmity with God? Therefore, whoever wants to be a lover of the world makes himself an enemy of God."

(James 4:4)

A "lover of the world" is someone who seeks after only the passing pleasures that this world has to offer at the expense of integrity and the service of God and humanity. A person becomes an enemy of God when he lets himself be controlled by his destructive tendencies.

"The concern of the flesh is death, but the concern of the Spirit is life and peace. For the concern of the flesh is hostility toward God; it does not submit to the law of God, nor can it; and those who are in the flesh cannot please God." (Rom. 8:6-8)

I ask myself: What does St. Paul mean when he uses the terms, *"in the flesh"* and *"in the Spirit"*?

Living *"in the flesh"* in Scripture means living without God's presence and help in our lives. Leaving God out of our choices results in our choosing selfishness and the opposite of God's ways. On the other hand, living *"in the Spirit"* means living with God's presence and help in our lives.

Prayer

"For day and night Your hand was heavy upon me; my strength was sapped as in the heat of summer. Then I acknowledged my sin to You and did not cover up my iniquity. I said, I will confess my transgressions to the Lord – and You forgave the guilt of my sin."

(Psalm 32: 4-5)

Tuesday of the Second Week of Lent

The Problem of Evil

"Your throne, O God, will last forever and ever; a scepter of justice will be the scepter of your kingdom. You love justice and hate iniquity, therefore God, your God, has set you above your companions by anointing you with the oil of joy." (Psalm 45: 6-7)

If we do not believe in the justice of God, then all human attempts to make sense of the evils we all must face fail. The justice of God is our joy. Or as Dante said in the 1300's when he entered heaven in his depiction of Paradise: "In Your will is our peace."

(Dante, Canto III of the Paradiso)

Seeking the peace that comes from a right relationship with God comes from being invested in the "justice of God." To seek the justice of God is to come out of our self-sufficiency and recognize our poverty before God, our need for God and God's ways.

"Blessed are the poor in spirit, for theirs is the kingdom of heaven." (Matt. 5:3)

To seek justice is to undergo a conversion of heart, to make a decision about evil: I will no longer justify myself. I will no longer live as others live. I will not do what everyone does. I will not feel justified in ambiguous, dubious and evil actions just because others do the same. I will now begin to see my life through the eyes of God. I will look for the good, even if I find it uncomfortable. I will no longer direct my life at the judgment of the majority, or of other people I esteem, but I will direct my life at the justice of God.

The essence of Christ's message is not merely doing the right things and avoiding the wrong things. It is the gift of a new friendship, the gift of communion with Jesus and thereby with God. The largest step for someone to make in order to come to terms with the evil in their own hearts is to make this decision: I cannot build my own goodness through my own strengths. I need God.

I ask myself: What injustice, what evil do I see in my own life?

Prayer

Lord Jesus Christ, Lord of eternal life, full right to pass definitive judgment on the works and hearts of all people belongs to You as redeemer of the world. You "acquired" this right by Your cross. The Father has given "all judgment to the Son." Yet You did not come to judge, but to save and to give the life You have in Yourself. Bring us to a greater awareness that by rejecting grace in this life, one already judges oneself, receives according to one's works, and can even condemn oneself for all eternity by rejecting the Spirit of love. Help us always remember that on the Last Day, You, Lord Jesus, will say: *"Truly I say to you, as you did it to one of the least of these my brethren, you did it to me."* In Your Holy Name, I pray. Amen.

Wednesday of the Second Week of Lent

The Problem of Evil

Taking a close look at our own time, we can see, if we are open to the prompting of the Holy Spirit, a powerful and convicting description of the problem of evil in our times in St. Paul's Letter to the Romans.

"The wrath of God is indeed being revealed from heaven against every impiety and wickedness of those who suppress the truth by their wickedness.

"For what can be known about God is evident to them, because God made it evident to them. Ever since the creation of the world, his invisible attributes of eternal power and divinity have been able to be understood and perceived in what he has made. As a result, they have no excuse; for although they knew God they did not accord him glory as God or give him thanks. Instead, they became vain in their reasoning, and their senseless minds were darkened.

"While claiming to be wise, they became fools and exchanged the glory of the immortal God for the likeness

of an image of mortal man or of birds or of four-legged animals or of snakes.

"*Therefore, God handed them over to impurity through the lusts of their hearts for the mutual degradation of their bodies. They exchanged the truth of God for a lie and revered and worshiped the creature rather than the creator, who is blessed forever. Amen.*

"*Therefore, God handed them over to degrading passions. Their females exchanged natural relations for unnatural, and the males likewise gave up natural relations with females and burned with lust for one another. Males did shameful things with males and thus received in their own persons the due penalty for their perversity.*

"*And since they did not see fit to acknowledge God, God handed them over to their undiscerning mind to do what is improper. They are filled with every form of wickedness, evil, greed, and malice; full of envy, murder, rivalry, treachery, and spite. They are gossips and scandalmongers and they hate God. They are insolent, haughty, boastful, ingenious in their wickedness, and rebellious toward their parents. They are senseless, faithless, heartless, ruthless. Although they know the just decree of God that all who practice such things deserve death, they not only do them but give approval to those who practice them."*

(Romans 1: 18-32)

I ask myself: How does this Scripture make me feel?

Prayer

Lord, this Scripture is hard to hear in our time. Our whole world seems to reject the message in this Scripture. However, we have come to believe that You have the words of eternal life. Open my mind to listen to Your voice; and help me see how You are a God of love and a God of justice at the same time. In Your Holy Name I pray. Amen.

Thursday of the Second Week of Lent

The Problem of Evil

"No discipline seems pleasant at the time, but painful. Later on, however, it produces a harvest of righteousness and peace for those who have been trained by it." (Hebrews 12:11)

Justice always includes the notion of there being a consequence for deeds that violate justice. The New Testament calls this consequence the "Wrath of God." Yet, we believe in a God of love. How, then shall we understand the punishment of God, or the "Wrath of God"?

Here is the teaching on this by the man who is now Pope: "Punishment is the situation in which man finds himself if he has alienated himself from his own essential being . . . .

"The wrath of God is a way of saying that I have been living in a way that is contrary to the love that is God. Anyone who begins to live and grow away from God, who lives away from what is good, is turning his life toward wrath. Whoever falls away from love is moving into negativity.

"So that is not something that some dictator with a lust for power inflicts on you, but is simply a way of expressing the inner logic of a certain action. If I move outside the area of what is compatible with the ideal model by which I am created, if I move beyond the love that sustains me, well then, I just fall into the void, into darkness. I am then no longer in the realm of love, so to speak, but in a realm that can be seen as the realm of wrath.

"When God inflicts punishment, this is not punishment in the sense that God has, as it were, drawn up a system of fines and penalties and is wanting to pin one on you. 'The punishment of God' is in fact an expression for having missed the right road and then experiencing the consequences that follow from taking the wrong track and wandering away from the right way of living . . . .

"It is important that the Church should draw a large enough image of God and not decorate it with artificial dreadful threats . . . ."

Joseph Cardinal Ratzinger
Address to Catechists and Religion Teachers,
Jubilee of Catechists, 12 December 2000

I ask myself: What consequences have I seen from some poor choices I have made?

Prayer

Lord God, thank You for drawing us, even as we tremble, into the mystery of Your love and Your justice, for in You justice and peace shall kiss. Help us see more clearly that in justice there are consequences of our choices, for good or for ill. Show us the way so that we may not move away from Your love. Help us so that we do not become wrathful, negative persons, but always open to Your love. In the Name of Jesus.

Friday of the Second Week of Lent

The Problem of Evil

"This is the definition of sin: the misuse of powers given us by God for doing good, a use contrary to God's Commandments."

The Detailed Rules for Monks
Basil the Great (d. 379 A.D.)

If I am totally honest with myself, I know that I am, like the rest of humanity, a perpetrator of some injustice. In some specific ways I have misused the powers God has given me to do good. I also know that I can easily see the sins of others but have more difficulty in seeing my own sins.

"Sin directs the heart of the wicked; their eyes are closed to the fear of God. For they live with the delusion: their guilt will not be known and hated. Empty and false are the words of their mouth; they have ceased to be wise and do good. In their beds they hatch plots; they set out on a wicked way; they do not reject evil."

(Psalm 36: 1-5)

How do we know what leads us to God and what leads us away from God?

"Keep, then, my statutes and decrees, for the man who carries them out will find life through them."

(Leviticus 18:5)

God revealed His Law, including the Ten Commandments, through Moses at Mount Sinai. In doing so, God gave human beings His own insight into what will make us happy and what will destroy us.

"The Lord set knowledge before human beings, he endowed them with the law of life. He established an eternal covenant with them and revealed his judgments to them." (Sirach/Ecclesiasticus 17:9-10)

There is, however, for Catholics a fuller sense of the "Law" beyond the Ten Commandments. It includes the whole Judaeo-Christian ethic of social justice and service to the needy.

"If you put an end to oppression, to every gesture of contempt, and to every evil word; if you give food to the hungry and satisfy those who are in need, then the darkness around you will turn to the brightness of noon."

(Isaiah 58:9-10)

I ask myself: On what specific attitude or action, do I need to repent?

A Lenten Friday's Formal Act of Repentance

Help me, Lord, on this Lenten Friday to understand that others' sins, the ones I most get enraged by, are telling me something about my own need of repentance. Help me, Lord, to see myself the way You see me: absolutely loved, but also very much a sinner. Help me see myself the way You see me, for when You show me my sins, I am not destroyed by them, but filled with confident trust in Your grace and mercy to renew me and make me whole.

Suggestion: Go to the Sacrament of Reconciliation

Saturday of the Second Week of Lent

Transition from the Problem
To the Solution to the Problem

"For we did not heed the voice of the Lord, our God, in all the words of the prophets whom he sent us, but each one of us went off after the devices of our own wicked hearts, served other gods, and did evil in the sight of the Lord, our God." (Baruch 1:21-22)

If I do not own my own sinfulness and recognize that I, too, need a Savior, then I will be walking in the darkness, trying to save myself, justifying my own behaviors, and wanting the rest of the world to call my sin "good."

"Woe to those who call evil good and good evil, who put darkness for light, and light for darkness, who put bitter for sweet and sweet for bitter." (Isaiah 5: 20)

If I own my sinfulness, then it will be easier for me to avoid the temptation to diminish Jesus Christ, the Son of God, into a merely historical Jesus, into a mere man. If I see my own infidelities accurately, I will not want to distill from the Bible a Jesus to my own size, a Jesus who goes along with my self-deceptions.

"The opposite of salvation is . . . the definitive suffering: the loss of eternal life, being rejected by God, damnation."

SALVIFICI DOLORIS, No. 14, Feb. 1984,

by Pope John Paul II

Judgment

I ask myself: Do I really think I owe an accounting for my choices in life?

Man will be judged. He must account for things. This certitude is of value both for the powerful as well as the simple ones. Where this is honored, the limitations of every power in this world are traced. God renders justice, and only he may ultimately do this. We will be able to do this better the more we are able to live under the eyes of God and to communicate the truth of justice to the world. Thus the article of faith in justice, its force in the formation of consciences, is a central theme of the Gospel and is truly good news. It is for all those suffering the injustices of the world and who are looking for justice.

This is also how we can understand the connection between the Kingdom of God and the "poor," the suffering and all those spoken about in the Beatitudes in the Speech on the Mountain. They are protected by the certainty of judgment, by the certitude, that there is a justice.

This is the true content of the article on justice, about God as judge: Justice exists. The injustices of the world are not the final word of history. Justice exists. Only whoever does not want there to be justice can oppose this truth.

Joseph Cardinal Ratzinger,
Address to Catechists and Religion Teachers,
Jubilee of Catechists, 12 December 2000

Prayer

Lord, Jesus Christ, Son of God, have mercy on me a sinner. (The Jesus Prayer)

The Third Sunday of Lent

The Solution to the Problem of Evil: Jesus Christ

"For in [Christ Jesus] all the fullness of God was pleased to dwell, and through him God was pleased to reconcile to himself all things, whether on earth or in heaven, by making peace through the blood of his cross."

(Colossians 1:19-20)

Since God loves us and wants us to be happy, God has a solution for all the causes of our unhappiness. Jesus Christ is the solution to all the problems in life: sin, suffering and death.

The mystery of God's solution to the problem of evil is called:

REDEMPTION

The redemption of the world – this tremendous mystery of love in which creation is renewed – is, at its deepest root, the fullness of justice in a human Heart – the Heart of the First-born Son – in order that it may become justice in the hearts of many human beings, predestined from eternity in the Firstborn Son to be children of God and called to grace, called to love.

(John Paul II, *Redemptor Hominis,* No. 9)

Remember that human beings made the free choice to be at enmity with God. God, however, took the initiative through His Son to make peace with us and restore us to His friendship. Even when God, who is love, became flesh in Jesus Christ, we continued to choose to be at enmity with God. We even crucified Him. Despite our rejection, He had this attitude of love toward all of us:

"Father, forgive them, for they know not what they do."

(Luke 23:34)

I ask myself: Am I willing to walk this earth in the manner of my Redeemer?

Prayer

Eternal Lord of all things, I feel Your gaze on me.

I sense that Your Mother stands near,

and the great beings crowd around You,

angels and powers and martyrs and saints.

If You will help me, please,

I would like to make an offering:

I want it to be my desire, and my choice,

provided that You want it this way,

to walk this earth the way You walked it.

I know that You lived in a little town,

without luxury, without great education.

I know that You refused political power.

I know that You suffered: Leaders rejected You.

Friends abandoned you. You failed.

I know. I hate to think about it.

None of it looks romantic to me, or very useful.

But it seems to me a toweringly wonderful thing

that Your divine majesty might call me

to follow after You. Amen

(from *Choosing Christ in the World,*

by Joseph Tetlow, S.J.)

Monday of the Third Week of Lent

The Solution: Jesus Christ

Peoples everywhere, open the doors to Christ! His Gospel in no way detracts from man's freedom, from the respect that is owed to every culture and to whatever is good in each religion. By accepting Christ, you open yourselves to the definitive Word of God, to the One in whom God has made himself fully known and has shown us the path to himself.

(John Paul II, *Redemptoris Missio*, No. 3)

How is Jesus Christ the solution to the problem of evil?

"The Incarnation tells us something about God and something about ourselves: that God is love, and that we are the object of God's love. God is greater than our sin, greater than the ways we become alienated, greater than all shortcomings at every time in history and in every place on earth, because God is love, and that love was most sublimely proven on Calvary. When we freely choose to enter into the mystery of God's love, and accept it, we become transformed and redeemed, set free from our fears, and we realize that our God has made us rulers and caretakers of the whole created order.

"However, the temptation today is to reduce Christianity to a merely human wisdom, a pseudo-science of well-being. In our heavily secularized world a 'gradual secularization of salvation' has taken place, so that people strive for the material good of human beings;" but what winds up happening is a reducing of the value of the human person to a truncated version of a human being, leaving no concern for his heavenly future. "The moral and spiritual dimensions are ignored and stifled. We know, however, that Jesus came to bring a salvation that embraces the whole person and all of humankind.

"Without this salvation of the whole person, and the whole of humanity, modern human beings live in an increasing state of fear, even terror, with the greatest fear being, an unimaginable self-destruction, compared with which all the cataclysms and catastrophes of history known to us seek to fade away."

(John Paul II, *Redemptor Hominis,* No. 15)

"The answer to humanity's fear of itself lay in rediscovering that human nature is moral and spiritual, not simply material."

Witness to Hope, the Biography of Pope John Paul II,

by George Weigel

"It is by God's will that we have been sanctified through the offering of the body of Jesus Christ once and for all." (Hebrews 10:10)

I ask myself: Am I getting the picture that the way of Jesus is the way of love?

Prayer

Welcome, Lord Jesus Christ, into our flesh, into the heart of humanness. I welcome Your godly holiness upon earth. I welcome Your complete humanness upon my life . . . I welcome You, Yourself, into my life and self. I thank You that I may embrace humanity and find myself embracing You. For You remain in our flesh now and forever, among humankind whose eyes reflect Your eyes, whose use of words matches Your use of words, whose need of You matches Your willing need of us.

(Adapted from *Choosing Christ in the World*, by Joseph Tetlow, S.J.)

Tuesday of the Third Week of Lent

The Solution: Jesus Christ

"Through his suffering, my servant shall justify many, and their guilt he shall bear . . . . Therefore I will give him his portion among the great, and he shall divide the spoils with the mighty, because he surrendered himself to death and was counted among the wicked; and he shall take away the sins of many, and win pardon for their offenses." (Isaiah 53: 11-12)

One might reasonably ask why Jesus had to die on the cross. Why could He not have simply declared us all forgiven and that we were God's friends again?

Jesus' death on the cross makes clear how terrible is our rejection of God and of goodness. God the Father's decision to let His Son die on the cross proves how seriously He takes sin.

"There are six things the Lord hates, yes, seven are an abomination to him; haughty eyes, a lying tongue, and hands that shed innocent blood; a heart that plots wicked schemes, feet that run swiftly to evil, the false

witness who utters lies, and he who sows discord among brothers." (Proverbs 6: 16-19)

The reason God hates sin so much is because God knows that sin causes great suffering to ourselves and to others. *"Those who commit sin and do evil bring harm on themselves."* (Tobit 12:10)

So, though we are deserving of condemnation and we freely condemn each other, we are instead brought into the mercy of God by our acceptance of His freely offered gift of salvation in Christ Jesus. *"There is therefore no condemnation for those who are in Christ Jesus. For the law of the Spirit of life in Christ Jesus has set you free from the law of sin and of death."* (Romans 8:1-2)

"Man cannot live without love. He remains a being that is incomprehensible for himself, his life is senseless, if love is not revealed to him, if he does not encounter love, if he does not experience it and make it his own, if he does not participate intimately in it. This, as has already been said, is why Christ the Redeemer "fully reveals man to himself". If we may use the expression, this is the human dimension of the mystery of the Redemption. In this dimension man finds again the greatness, dignity and value that belong to his humanity. (John Paul II, *Redemptor Hominis*, No. 10)

I ask myself: Am I getting the picture that the way of Jesus is the way of the Cross?

Prayer before a Crucifix

Look down upon me, good and gentle Jesus, while before Your face I humbly kneel, and with a burning soul pray and beseech You to fix deep in my heart lively sentiments of faith, hope and charity, true contrition for my sins, and a firm purpose of amendment, while I contemplate Your five wounds, pondering over them within me, calling to mind the words which David, Your prophet, said of You, my good Jesus: *"They have pierced my hands and my feet; they have numbered all my bones."* (Psalm 21:17-18)

Wednesday of the Third Week of Lent

The Solution: Jesus Christ

"This man, delivered up by the set plan and fore-knowledge of God, you killed, using lawless men to crucify him. But God raised him up, releasing him from the throes of death, because it was impossible for him to be held by it. For David says of him: 'I saw the Lord ever before me, with him at my right hand I shall not be disturbed. Therefore my heart has been glad and my tongue has exulted; my flesh, too, will dwell in hope."

(Acts 2: 23-26)

We might reasonably ask what proof there would be that the Cross of Jesus made us friends again with God. The proof of Jesus Christ's victory over the problem of evil is His resurrection from the dead. That means, as well, that He is alive and in our midst today and offers us the same friendship He offered the Apostles. As the Risen Lord said to St. Thomas the Apostle, referring to us: *"Put your finger here and see my hands. Reach out your hand and put it in my side. Do not*

67

doubt but believe." Thomas answered him, "My Lord and my God!" Jesus said to him, "Have you believed because you have seen me? Blessed are those who have not seen and yet have come to believe." (John 20:27-29)

"Church's proclamation of Jesus Christ, *'the way, the truth, and the life'* (Jn 14:6), today also makes use of the practice of inter-religious dialogue. Such dialogue certainly does not replace, but rather accompanies the mission to the Gentiles, directed toward that – mystery of unity – from which, it follows that all men and women who are saved share, though differently, in the same mystery of salvation in Jesus Christ through his Spirit."

Dominus Iesus, No. 2, August 6, 2000

In other words, "It must therefore be firmly believed as a truth of Catholic faith that the universal salvific will of the One and Triune God is offered and accomplished once for all in the mystery of the incarnation, death, and resurrection of the Son of God."

Dominus Iesus, No. 14, August 6, 2000

I ask myself: Can I wrap my mind around the truth that salvation means the Father seeing in us what He sees and loves in His Son, Jesus Christ?

Prayer

So great was your love

that you gave us Your Son as our redeemer.

You sent him as one like ourselves,

though free from sin,

that you might see and love in us

what you see and love in Christ.

Your gifts of grace, lost by disobedience,

are now restored in the obedience of your Son.

(Preface VII for Sundays in Ordinary Time)

Thursday of the Third Week of Lent

The Solution: Jesus Christ

"I have been put to death with Christ on his cross, so that it is no longer I who live, but it is Christ who lives in me. This life I live now, I live by faith in the Son of God, who loved me and gave his life for me."

(Galatians 2:19-20)

What benefit is there for those who come to believe in Jesus?

All who believe in Jesus, crucified and risen from the dead, are reconciled to God, made friends with God, put right with God. They understand what it means to be forgiven; and Christ dwells within them.

"Paul [in his Letter to the Ephesians] amasses all of these Old Testament images to show us who we are as Christ's body, the Church. We are now the commonwealth of Israel. We are now no longer strangers to the covenants of promise; we are now the heirs to the covenant promises. We are now members of the household of faith. We are now sons and daughters of God the Father. We are no longer strangers and sojourners; we are now, with the apostles and the prophets, living stones making up a holy temple so that practically everything in the Old Testament which manifests the splendor and glory of God is our birthright. That's who the Church is – that's who you are – as members of Christ's Mystical Body. We are the mystery of Christ because Christ dwells within us; His body and His blood dwell within us."

The Splendor of the Church, by Scott Hahn

If we are not restored to God's friendship, we continue to be slaves of our destructive tendencies and we continue to choose selfishness, which is the root cause of our unhappiness. *"When you were servants of sin, you felt no obligation to uprightness, and what did you gain from living like that? Experiences of which you are now ashamed, for that sort of behavior ends in death."* (Romans 6:20-21)

I ask myself: Do I understand yet how I, specifically I, need a savior?

Father William E. Breslin

Prayer

"Have mercy on me, God, in your goodness;
in your abundant compassion blot out my offense.
Turn away your face from my sins; blot out all my guilt.
A clean heart create for me, God;
renew in me a steadfast spirit.
Do not drive me from your presence,
nor take from me your holy spirit.
Restore my joy in your salvation;
sustain in me a willing spirit.
I will teach the wicked your ways,
that sinners may return to you.
Rescue me from death, God, my saving God,
that my tongue may praise your healing power.
Lord, open my lips; my mouth will proclaim your praise."

(Psalm 51:3, 11-17)

Friday of the Third Week of Lent

The Solution: Jesus Christ

"None of the trials which have come upon you is more than a human being can stand. You can trust that God will not let you be put to the test beyond your strength, but with any trial will also provide a way out by enabling you to put up with it." (1Corinthians 10:13)

Suffering

The way Christ Jesus saves us during the sufferings we face in life is to help us unite our sufferings with the sufferings of Christ. If we remember how the Lord has loved us through all previous suffering, we will surely find patience to endure the present suffering.

"Remember the days past when, after you had been enlightened, you endured a great contest of suffering. At times you were publicly exposed to abuse and affliction; at other times you associated yourselves with those so treated. You even joined in the sufferings of

those in prison and joyfully accepted the confiscation of your property, knowing that you had a better and lasting possession. Therefore, do not throw away your confidence; it will have great recompense. You need endurance to do the will of God and receive what he has promised. 'For, after just a brief moment, he who is to come shall come; he shall not delay. But my just one shall live by faith, and if he draws back I take no pleasure in him.' We are not among those who draw back and perish, but among those who have faith and will possess life." (Hebrews 10: 32-39)

There is a reward for our patience in suffering and for uniting our sufferings with the sufferings of Christ: It's love!

"In suffering 'man is forced to face the fact that existence is not at his disposal, nor is his life his own property.' Man can respond either in anger to this reality or choose the Christian approach in which: 'man can respond by seeking to trust this strange power to Whom he is subject. He can allow himself to be led, unafraid, by the hand, without Angst-ridden concern for his situation. And in this second case [or response], the human attitude towards pain, towards the presence of death within living, merges with the attitude we call love.'"

Joseph Ratzinger,

Eschatology: Death and Eternal Life, 1977, p. 96

I ask myself: Do I find this Christian meaning in my sufferings; or I am I more of a stoic with the attitude of "grin and bear it"?

A Lenten Friday's Prayer on the Suffering of Christ

Lord Jesus Christ,

Did I know how I would break my heart with grief for You? Of all the people in the world, You should have suffered the least. I am ashamed of what we did to You while You broke Your heart with grief for me.

Saturday of the Third Week of Lent

Transition from Knowing the Solution
To Implementing the Solution

"For we know that when this tent we live in – our body here on earth – is torn down, God will have a house in heaven for us to live in, a home he himself has made, which will last forever." (2 Corinthians 5:1)

The final suffering is death. Yet, Jesus Christ and His resurrection reveal to us that God's love for us is not for this life only. When this life is done, those who have died in Christ have a home in heaven.

Therefore, Jesus Christ is the solution to every problem in this life and at death. And we call this:

Salvation

"I am the way and the truth and the life. No one comes to the Father except through me." (John 14:6)

Heaven

"Those who die in God's grace and friendship and are perfectly purified live forever with Christ. They are like God, for they 'see him as he is,' face to face . . . . This perfect life with the Most Holy Trinity – this communion of life and love with the Trinity, with the Virgin Mary, the angels and all the blessed – is called 'heaven.' Heaven is the ultimate end and fulfillment of the deepest human longings, the state of supreme, definitive happiness."

(Catechism of the Catholic Church, No. 1023-1024)

I ask myself: Do I yearn for heaven? Do I keep heaven before me as my ultimate goal? Or do I have lurking in my heart an underlying attitude that I do not need to be saved?

"Jesus scandalized the Pharisees by eating with tax collectors and sinners as familiarly as with themselves. Against those among them *'who trusted in themselves that they were righteous and despised others,'* Jesus affirmed: *'I have not come to call the righteous, but sinners to repentance.'* He went further by proclaiming before the Pharisees that, *'since sin is universal, those who pretend not to need salvation are blind to themselves.'"*

(Catechism of the Catholic Church, No. 588)

A Lenten Act of Hope

Good Jesus, in You alone I place all my hope.

You are my salvation and my strength, the Source of all good. Through Your mercy, and through Your passion and death, I hope to obtain the pardon of my sins, the grace of final perseverance and eternal happiness in heaven.

The Fourth Sunday of Lent

There Needs to Be a Response to the Solution: Jesus Christ

"Return to the Lord and give up sin, pray to him and make your offences few. Turn again to the Most High and away from sin, hate intensely what he loathes."

(Sirach 17:20-21)

If Jesus Christ is the solution to every problem, then there must be something we must do to experience this "salvation." What response must we give to Jesus?

Our response to God's offer of salvation in Christ is fourfold:

1. Undergo a change of attitude toward God and God's ways;
2. Make a commitment to Jesus Christ;
3. Accept the Gift of the Holy Spirit; and
4. Embrace His Church.

Sacramentally we make these four responses through the Sacraments of Initiation (Baptism, Confirmation and the Eucharist) and the occasional use of the Sacrament of Reconciliation. However, for way too many Catholics these sacraments are not appreciated profoundly for what they are intended to do for us. Subsequently, many Catholics are not brought to Christian maturity but remain at an undeveloped level of faith. One telltale sign of needing still to grow to Christian maturity is resentment against God or His ways or His church.

"In this world the Church is a mixed community and will stay that way until the end – unthreshed corn, the ark with both clean and unclean animals, a ship full of unruly passengers who always seem to be on the point of wrecking it . . . . Even the best of her children are themselves never any more than in the way of sanctification, and their sanctity is always liable to shipwreck; all alike have to flee from the evil of the times to the mercy of God. Thus it is that the Church which we are must say daily, as with one voice and without exception: 'And forgive us our trespasses.'"

Henri de Lubac,

The Splendor of the Church, 1999, pp. 112-115

I ask myself: Am I willing to make a more authentic response to the salvation God offers me in Christ?

Prayer

You are the irresistible and vivifying force, O Lord, and because yours is the energy, because, of the two of us, you are infinitely the stronger, it is on you that falls the part of consuming me in the union that should weld us together. Vouchsafe, therefore, something more precious still than the grace for which all the faithful pray. It is not enough that I should die while communicating. Teach me to treat my death as an act of communion.

Pierre Teilhard de Chardin, *The Divine Milieu,* p. 89

Monday of the Fourth Week of Lent

Our Fourfold Response
Part One: A Change of Attitude

"I was ready to respond to those who asked me not, to be found by those who sought me not. I said: Here I am! Here I am! To a nation that did not call on my name. I have stretched out my hands all the day to a rebellious people, who walk in evil paths and follow their own thoughts." (Isaiah 65:1-2)

A change of attitude toward God and God's ways is called a "conversion of heart." It means honestly facing the destructiveness of our sins and wanting Jesus to make our lives better. This means giving up sin. But how?

We give up sin by: admitting specifically the sins that keep us at a distance from God; admitting that we need God; asking Jesus to save us (especially if we are caught in a sinful thought pattern or behavior or relation ship from which we cannot seem to extricate ourselves).

I ask myself: OK, if I admit my sinfulness, can I on my own make my life better?

No. We cannot on our own rid our lives of our vices. We must admit that we need God. This attitude of not admitting that we need God is the chief reason we do not grow.

So, submit yourselves to God. *"Resist the devil, and he will flee from you. Draw near to God, and he will draw near to you. Cleanse your hands, you sinners, and purify your hearts, you of two minds. Humble your-selves before the Lord and he will exalt you."*

(James 4:7-8, 10)

Father William E. Breslin

Prayer

Lord, by virtue of Your very perfections, You cannot ordain that the elements of a world in the course of growth – or at least of a fallen world in the process of rising again – should avoid shocks and diminishments, even moral ones. But You will make it good – You will take Your revenge, if one may use the expression – by making evil itself serve a higher good of Your faithful, the very evil which the present state of creation does not allow You to suppress immediately. Like an artist who is able to make use of a fault or an impurity in the stone he is sculpting or the bronze he is casting so as to produce more exquisite lines or a more beautiful tone, You, without sparing us the partial deaths, nor the final death, which form an essential part of our lives, transfigure them by integrating them in a better plan – provided we lovingly trust in You. Not everything is immediately good to those who seek You, God; but everything is capable of becoming good.

Adapted from Pierre Teilhard de Chardin,
The Divine Milieu, p. 85.

Tuesday of the Fourth Week of Lent

Our Fourfold Response
Part Two: A Commitment to Jesus Christ

"Brothers, what should we do? Peter said to them, Repent and be baptized, every one of you in the name of Jesus Christ so that your sins may be forgiven; and you will receive the gift of the Holy Spirit. For the promise is for you, for your children, and for all who are far away, everyone whom the Lord our God calls to him."

(Acts 2:38-39)

Committing our lives to Christ is the most crucial step to take towards Christian maturity, but many of the baptized skip it and move on to Holy Communion without ever coming into a deep relationship with the Lord of our salvation.

"An awareness needs to develop that in fact to a large extent, we no longer know Christianity at all. For example, how many images in a church no longer say anything to some people? The original meaning is no longer generally understood . . . . Nevertheless, the predominant mentality is still that we already know all about Christianity and are now in search of something different. There needs to be a renewal of what you could call a curiosity about Christianity, the desire really to discover what it's all about. It would be very important for preachers to show the way out of this feeling of staleness, this feeling that we are already long familiar with it, to create curiosity about the richness hidden in Christianity, so that this richness is regarded no longer as a matter of burdensome systems, but as a living treasure that is worth knowing.

Joseph Cardinal Ratzinger,

in the 1997 interview, *Salt of the Earth*

I ask myself: How do I commit my life to Christ?

With a Prayer Such as This, Genuinely Prayed:

I choose to breathe the Breath of Christ that makes all life holy. I choose to live the flesh of Christ that outlasts sin's corrosion and decay. I choose the Blood of Christ along my veins and in my heart that dizzies me with joy. I choose the living waters flowing from His side to wash clean my own self and the world itself. I choose the awful agony of Christ to charge my senseless sorrows with meaning and to make my pain pregnant with power. I choose You, good Jesus, You know. I choose You, Good Lord; count me among the victories that You have won in bitter woundedness. Never number me among those alien to You. Make me safe from all that seeks to destroy me. Summon me to come to You. Stand me solid among angels and saints chanting yes to all You have done, exulting in all You mean to do forever and ever. Then for this time, Father of all, keep me, from the core of myself, choosing Christ in the world. Amen.

Joseph Tetlow, S.J., *Choosing Christ in the World*

Wednesday of the Fourth Week of Lent

Our Fourfold Response
Part Three: Accepting the Gift of the Holy Spirit

"You shall receive power when the Holy Spirit comes upon you, and you will be my witnesses . . . to the ends of the earth." (Acts 1:8)

In the Sacrament of Confirmation we are "sealed with the Gift of the Holy Spirit," as we are anointed on our foreheads with Sacred Chrism. This gift of the Holy Spirit empowers us to give witness to Christ by our lives; we are given the courage and wisdom to say or do what is right and just, no matter what the cost; and we are inspired to live out our baptismal vocation of being a presence of Christ daily in all that we say and do.

But how seriously do we take our Confirmation? And how seriously do we take our Baptism, which most of us received when we were babies?

So, let us now, this Lent, take our Baptism and our Confirmation seriously by yielding control of our lives over to the Spirit of Jesus. For when we yield control of our lives over to the Spirit of Jesus, we are empowered to move beyond our personal rendition of who Jesus is and embrace the Church who gives us the true Jesus Christ. For the head of the Church is Jesus Christ. *"From whom the whole body, supported and held together by its ligaments and bonds, achieves the growth that comes from God."* (Colossians 2:19)

I ask myself: What image can I use to help me see the Spirit filling me?

"Let's suppose that you must fill a sack. Realizing that what will be given to you is very great, you stretch the opening of the sack or bag or whatever kind of container it is, as much as you can. You know how much you have to put in it, and you see that it's small. So, by stretching it, you make it capable of holding more. In the same way, God, by deferring our hope, stretches our desire; by the desiring, stretches the mind, by stretching, makes it more capable of receiving.

Let us desire, therefore, my brethren, for we shall be filled.

St Augustine,
Commentary on the First Letter of John

Prayer to Mary, Cherished Spouse of the Holy Spirit

O Mary, worthy Spouse of the Holy Spirit and beloved Mother of my soul, who from the first moment of Your existence were adorned with the Gifts of the Holy Spirit and made them bear admirable fruits by a constant fidelity and an ever-increasing love, please cast a glance of compassion upon Your child, so poor and unworthy, as I kneel here at Your feet. O Mary pray for me to live by the Gifts of the Spirit: the Fear of the Lord, Piety, Knowledge, Fortitude, Counsel, Understanding, and Wisdom, which will help me know where true happiness lies.

Thursday of the Fourth Week of Lent

Our Fourfold Response
Part Four: Embracing the Church

"Husbands, love your wives, even as Christ loved the church and handed himself over for her to sanctify her, cleansing her by the bath of water with the word, that he might present to himself the church in splendor, without spot or wrinkle or any such thing, that she might be holy and without blemish. So (also) husbands should love their wives as their own bodies. He who loves his wife loves himself. For no one hates his own flesh but rather nourishes and cherishes it, even as Christ does the church, because we are members of his body."

(Ephesians 5:25-30)

Do you think there are many of the baptized who would prefer a disembodied Christ? A Christ who would prefer to stay in heaven, where everything is perfect? A Christ who would not associate with His Bride the Church? Yet read some of the wisdom of Cardinal Henri de Lubac who was one of the brightest stars among theologians of the last century:

"Love should, of course, be our only response to our Mother the Church; yet in fact there are many temptations that trouble us with regard to her. There are some that are perennial and some that are peculiar to our time, and they are all too varied – even to the point of mutual opposition – for any one of us ever to think himself sheltered from the threat they constitute. We must not relax in any way our zeal for Catholic truth, but we should learn how to purify it. We must be on guard against turning into those "carnal men" who have existed since the first generation of Christians and who, turning the Church into their own personal property, practically stopped the Apostles from announcing the Gospel to the Gentiles. For if we do that, we lay ourselves open to something yet more calamitous – collaboration with militant irreligion, by way of making it easier for it to carry out its self-assigned task of relegating the Church and her doctrine to the class of the defunct; we provide irreligion with a clear conscience, as it were, for it has no understanding of the actuality of the eternal."

Henri de Lubac,

The Splendor of the Church, 1999, pp. 112-115

I ask myself: Do I love the Church?

Prayer

O Lord Jesus Christ, You love Your bride, the Church, and You call us to love her as well. The mystery of the Church and the good things You give us through her are always beyond what we manage to live of them in actual practice. How patient You are! We never draw upon more than a meager part of the wealth that our Mother the Church has at her disposal. Yet, Lord, all Catholics who are not ingrates will have in their hearts that hymn of gratitude which has been given words by that great poet, Paul Claudel, "Praised be forever that great and majestic Mother at whose knees I have learned everything."

Friday of the Fourth Week of Lent

Our Fourfold Response
Part Four: Embracing the Church, continued

Jesus said, *"For where your treasure is, there your heart will be also."* (Matthew 6:21)

What are the treasures the Church offers us?

"The Church's deepest nature is expressed in her three-fold responsibility: of proclaiming the word of God, celebrating the sacraments, and exercising the ministry of charity. These duties presuppose each other and are inseparable."

Pope Benedict XVI, *Deus Caritas Est, No. 25*

Proclaiming the Word of God – Since everything asserted by the inspired authors or sacred writers must be held to be asserted by the Holy Spirit, it follows that the books of Scripture must be acknowledged as teaching solidly, faithfully and without error that truth which God wanted put into sacred writings for the sake of salvation.

Vatican II,

Dogmatic Constitution on Divine Revelation, No. 11

Celebrating the Sacraments – the purpose of the sacraments is to sanctify men, to build up the body of Christ, and, finally, to give worship to God. Because they are signs they also instruct. They not only presuppose faith, but by words and objects they also nourish, strengthen, and express it; that is why they are called "sacraments of faith."

Vatican II,

Constitution on the Sacred Liturgy, No. 59

Exercising the Ministry of Charity – for the Church, charity is not a kind of welfare activity which could equally well be left to others, but is a part of her nature, an indispensable expression of her very being.

Pope Benedict XVI, *Deus Caritas Est, No. 25*

I ask myself: Do I realize how much my life and my values are formed by the Gospel? Do I cherish enough the gifts God gives me in the sacraments; and do I take advantage of them frequently? And do I realize how central is my duty to be charitable?

A Lenten Friday's Prayer for
Valuing What Really Matters

Take, Lord, and receive
All my liberty, my memory, my understanding,
And my entire will —
All that I have and call my own.
You have given it all to me.
To You, Lord, I return it.
Everything is Yours now.
Do with it whatever You will.
Give me only Your love and Your grace.
That is enough for me.

Saturday of the Fourth Week of Lent

Transition from Response to Reward

"Behold I am coming soon! My reward is with me, and I will give to everyone according to what he has done. I am the Alpha and the Omega, the First and the Last, the Beginning and the End." (Revelation 22:12-13)

What is the reward for earnestly moving towards Christian maturity?

Heaven
How shall we describe heaven?

That's what we'll look at next week, the Fifth Week of Lent. But, know this: if we do not develop a strong sense of what heaven will be for us, it will slide to a less important consideration in our decisions and in our actions. Goal-setting is part of our culture, a very strong part of our culture. Yet, if we do not attend to our soul's goal then what will become of us?

"What good is it for anyone to gain the whole world, yet forfeit his soul? Or what can anyone give in exchange for his soul?" (Mark 8:36)

This is serious business because we can get waylaid and off onto a wrong path: *"Enter through the narrow gate; for the gate is wide and the road broad that leads to destruction, and those who enter through it are many. How narrow the gate and constricted the road that leads to life. And those who find it are few."*

(Matthew 7:13-14)

If, on the other hand, we keep our eyes fixed on the goal, then our whole lives will be filled with passion and clarity about why we are here, and where we are heading. It would also transform our experience of the Eucharist, as stated so beautifully by St John Chrysostom (347-407 AD):

A Eucharistic Reflection
As We Transition to Our Reward of Heaven

"Dearly beloved brothers and sisters, it's to our benefit to understand the miracle of the Eucharist – what the Gift is, why it was given, and what is its use. When we come back from that Table, we ought to be like so many lions breathing fire, dreadful to the devil. Our thoughts ought to be concentrated on our great Head and the love that he shows us . . . I feed you with my own Flesh, says the Lord, and join myself to you, desiring that you should all be children of noble blood now and giving you a noble hope of what you shall be hereafter . . . . Therefore, as the bearers of such a great mercy, let's watch our behavior."

The Fifth Sunday of Lent

The Reward of Christian Maturity

"Eye has not seen, and ear has not heard, nor has it entered the human heart, what God has prepared for those who love him." (1 Corinthians 2:9)

Heaven, how shall we describe it?

The reward for embracing the gifts the Lord has given to His Body the Church (the Scriptures, the Sacraments, and the Works of Charity) is heaven. And if we have heaven, eternal happiness, in mind always as our ultimate goal, we will find in this life a union with God that will transform our lives.

"Seek first the kingdom (of God) and his righteousness, and all these things [that the pagans seek] will be given you besides. Do not worry about tomorrow; tomorrow will take care of itself. Sufficient for a day is its own evil." (Matthew 6 31-34)

Having our eyes fixed on heaven colors everything we do in this life, even suffering. No one escapes suffering in this life, but it is transformed by our union with Jesus. Mother Teresa of Calcutta describes this transformation beautifully and succinctly: "The joy of suffering is the kiss of Jesus. Do not be afraid to share in that joy of suffering with Him because He will never give us more suffering than we are able to bear."

Blessed Theresa of Calcutta

St. Ignatius of Loyola taught that for us to taste heaven on earth, to ready ourselves for the joy of heaven and experience heaven on earth even in the midst of suffering, we must build our lives on what he called "The First Principal and Foundation." Let's use First Principal and Foundation as today's prayer:

The First Principal and Foundation of a Mature Christian's Life

We are created to praise, reverence and serve God, Our Lord, and by this means save our soul.

The other things on the face of the earth are created for us, and they are to aid us attain the purpose for which we are created.

Hence, we are to make use of them in as far as they help in the attainment of our end. Therefore, we must make ourselves indifferent to all created things, as far as we are allowed free choice and are not under any prohibition. Consequently, as far as we are concerned, we should not prefer health to sickness, riches to poverty, honor to dishonor, a long life to a short one. The same holds for all other things.

Our one desire and choice should be what is more conducive to the end for which we are created.

From *The Spiritual Exercises of St. Ignatius of Loyola*

Monday of the Fifth Week of Lent

The Reward of Christian Maturity

"I rejoice greatly in the Lord that now at last you revived your concern for me. You were, of course, concerned about me but lacked an opportunity. Not that I say this because of need, for I have learned, in whatever situation I find myself, to be self-sufficient. I know indeed how to live in humble circumstances; I know also how to live with abundance. In every circumstance and in all things I have learned the secret of being well fed and of going hungry, of living in abundance and of being in need. I have the strength for everything through him who empowers me." (Philippians 4: 10-13)

Another Reward of Christian Maturity: Holy Indifference

"Holy Indifference" is when I take a fundamental stance in life that says that I will never do anything to break my relationship with God; but I will choose only what my conscience freely allows me.

To get to this point we have to have made that leap of faith that God wants our welfare, not our woe, that He redeems us of all our past failures, that He calls us to an intimate relationship with Him. We need to have made as complete a response to Him as was capable for us so far, and we need to believe in the rewards He offers us. The result of all of this is "holy indifference." When we are given this gift, we will not try to tell God what will make us happy, but will wait to find out what God has been hoping us to accomplish by His grace in us and through us.

"Holding this kind of indifference among God's almost infinite number of gifts makes a person a great force for good. What a power she is who does not much care where she lives as long as God's hopes are being realized! What a power he is who does not much care whether he lives wealthy or not, only as long as God's justice is being done! Such a person truly finds God in all things – God creating, God raising up justice and peace in all things, God working busily so that no one will be lost, but everyone brought into the Reign."

Joseph A. Tetlow, S.J.,

Choosing Christ in the World, p. 131

I ask myself: Can I see "Holy Indifference" as something I might desire?

"Holy indifference" does not mean that we just sit back and wait for God to strike us the way He struck St. Paul on his way to Damascus. No, we still have to pray, think, and take counsel with trusted friends. We have to care about what the whole Church cares about and hopes for; and when our issues touch on matters addressed by the official teachers of the Church, i.e., the bishops and Pope; we must pay attention. But those with "holy indifference" will always be hoping to find God working within, leading our desires to be in conformity with His desires, shaping our lives and the world around us, and bringing the Kingdom of God to our reality.

Tuesday of the Fifth Week of Lent

The Reward of Christian Maturity

"The outcome or fruit of reading holy Scripture is by no means negligible: it is the fullness of eternal happiness. For these are the books that tell us of eternal life, which were written not only that we might believe but also that we might have everlasting life. When we do live that life we shall understand fully, we shall love completely, and our desires will be totally satisfied. Then, with all our needs fulfilled, we shall truly know the love that surpasses understanding and so be filled with the fullness of God."

St. Bonaventure, 1221 to 1274

Another Reward of Christian Maturity: Joy

Mother Teresa was asked this question: What is the most joyful place that you have ever visited? She answered, "Kalighat," which is a home for the dying, a hospital for the poor and sick in Calcutta, India, founded by Mother Teresa. "When the people die in peace, in the love of God, it is a wonderful thing. To see our poor people happy together with their families, these are beautiful things. The joy of the poor people is so clean, so clear. The real poor know what is joy."

The questioner persisted, "There are people who would say it is an illusion to think of the poor as joyous, that they must be given housing, raised up."

She answered, "The material is not the only thing that gives joy. Something greater than that, the deep sense of peace in the heart. They are content. That is the great difference between the rich and the poor."

I ask myself: Joy? Doesn't the Church, with all her commandments and prohibitions, turn to bitterness some of the most precious things in life? Doesn't she blow the whistle just when the joy gets going?

These were the questions of Friedrich Nietzsche, the German philosopher who paved the way psychologically for the Nazi Reich, and who accused the Church of having "poisoned" eros, a term to indicate "worldly" love, possessive love.

The mature Christian sees that it is the sickly eros of today that is poisoned. The love of Jesus is the medicine needed so much today. The gist of Pope

Benedict's Encyclical, *Deus Caritas Est*, is that God is impassioned like a lover for us, and is merciful to the point of dying for us, and that He is calling us back to grow in love, both with a healed eros and also a developed agape, which means a love grounded in and shaped by faith.

Prayer

God of love, true joy is found in working for justice and charity, in our love of You, and love of our neighbor. Help us see that the medicine of Your love, witnessed by the Church, is the world's most urgent need today.

Wednesday of the Fifth Week of Lent

The Reward of Christian Maturity

"What we are waiting for, relying on his promises, is the new heavens and new earth, where uprightness will be at home. So then, my dear friends, while you are waiting, do your best to live blameless and unsullied lives so that he will find you at peace. Think of his patience as your opportunity to be saved."

(2 Peter 3:13-15)

Another Reward of Christian Maturity: The Communion of Saints

Do you imagine heaven to be as thrilling as it will be? Do you ever wonder if we'll all get bored sitting around God's Throne? Do you think we'll grow tired of everything being perfect, and all our desires satisfied?

Most of us do not visualize heaven enough. We get so busy about our lives that the future, indeed the ultimate future, is on the back burner of our minds' occupations. We would do well, however, to be reminded of heaven every time we celebrate a sacrament, Mass, a Baptism, a Confirmation, a Wedding, a trip to the confessional, or the Anointing of the Sick, or an ordination. Look for the angels and saints. They are there! Just on the other side of being seen. They are our friends, our loved ones, the blessed, who are actively involved in our lives. We call this the "intercession of the saints" and our fellowship with them is called the "communion of saints."

"Being more closely united to Christ, those who dwell in heaven fix the Church more firmly in holiness. . . They do not cease to intercede with the Father for us, as they proffer the merits which they acquired on earth through the one mediator between God and men, Christ Jesus. . . So by their fraternal concern is our weakness greatly helped."

Lumen Gentium,
Vatican II, 1964

I ask myself: What is my vision of heaven?

Being an intercessor is what St. Dominic had in mind, when before he died in 1221 he said to his friars, "Do not weep, for I shall be more useful to you after my death and I shall help you then more effectively than during my life."

And who does not remember St. Therese of Lisieux, the Little Flower, saying before her death in 1897, "I want to spend my heaven doing good on earth."

Prayer: Think of a loved one who has died and pray

Saints of God, come to his/her aid. Receive his/her soul and present him/her to God Most High. May Christ, who called you, take you to himself, may angels lead you to Abraham's side. Receive his/her soul and present him/her to God Most High. Give him/her eternal rest, O Lord, and may your light shine on him/her for ever. Receive his/her soul and present him/her to God Most High.

Thursday of the Fifth Week of Lent

The Reward of Christian Maturity

"For my flesh is true food, and my blood is true drink. Whoever eats my flesh and drinks my blood remains in me and I in him. Just as the living Father sent me and I have life because of the Father, so also the one who feeds on me will have life because of me."

(John 6:55-57)

ONE WEEK FROM TODAY IS HOLY THURSDAY

Another Reward of Christian Maturity:
A Regular Taste of Heaven

The Eucharist is our weekly, daily if we want, encounter with heaven. We would do well when we enter church for Mass to imagine the angels and saints all gathered around the Throne of God, and at the Eucharist heaven opens up to us. In fact, heaven will come down upon our altar, and then be placed in our hands – so we can taste It.

"Ordinarily we cannot see or touch Jesus with our senses. But that is our limitation; not His. If we have eyes to see, **JESUS** is really now on earth in the Eucharist. Jesus is **REALLY** now on earth in the Eucharist. Jesus is really **NOW** on earth in the Eucharist. Jesus is really now **ON** earth in the Eucharist. Jesus is really now on **EARTH** in the Eucharist. Jesus is really now on earth **IN THE EUCHARIST**."

> John A. Hardon, SJ,
> *The Holy Eucharist is the Whole Christ*

"When the Church celebrates the Eucharist, the memorial of her Lord's death and resurrection, this central event of salvation becomes really present and 'the work of our redemption is carried out.' This sacrifice is so decisive for the salvation of the human race that Jesus Christ offered it and returned to the Father only after he had left us a means of sharing in it as if we had been present there. Each member of the faithful can thus take part in it and inexhaustibly gain its fruits. This is the faith from which generations of Christians down the ages have lived."

> John Paul II, Encyclical Letter,
> *Ecclesia de Eucharistia, 2003*

Re: The Mass: "I do not find Christians, outside of the catacombs, sufficiently sensible, aware, of conditions. Does anyone have the foggiest idea what sort of power we so blindly invoke? Or, as I suspect, does no one believe a word of it? The churches are children, playing on the floor with their chemistry sets, mixing up a batch of TNT to kill a Sunday morning."

Annie Dillard, *Holy the Firm,* 1977

Prayer

0 Lord, wean me away from the illusion of the comfort and permanence of earthly life. Purge my heart of any complacency when it comes to receiving the true bread come down from heaven. I cannot live without this bread and yet I am sometimes tempted to present myself at the altar not out of sincere desire, but perhaps more from pale routine and habit. This is not the way I wish to receive You, 0 Jesus. In the Eucharist, You give me a glimpse and a taste of heaven, my true and lasting home, where my restless heart longs to dwell with You for eternity. Amen.

Rev. Paul Check

Friday of the Fifth Week of Lent

Transition to Holy Week

"Behold, the life-giving cross on which was hung the salvation of the whole world. Oh, come, let us worship him. We adore you, O Christ, and we bless you. By your holy cross, you have redeemed the world."

Adoration of the Cross, Good Friday Liturgy

One week from today will be Good Friday

On Sunday, Palm Sunday, the Passion will be read at all Sunday Masses throughout the world. We thus begin the holiest week of the liturgical year. All Lent we have been studying and praying about becoming mature Christians. We are now ready to enter into Holy Week unlike ever before.

Readying ourselves for Holy Week

Holy Week is the time when the paschal mystery of the death, burial, and resurrection of Jesus Christ is celebrated bountifully. It is the heart of the Christian faith. The paschal mystery is celebrated every Sunday, the Lord's Day, as well as in every Eucharist; indeed, the entire liturgical life of the Church draws us into the redemptive work of Christ. The "ninety days" of Lent, Triduum, and Easter, the liturgical celebration of this paschal mystery, is a special moment of grace in the liturgical year.

Entering into the Pascal Mystery

The Pascal Mystery might not be a phrase that is familiar to all of you, it is a phrase that was coined by Augustine as he was trying to describe the Christ mystery. The mystery is that life and death, loss and renewal are the two sides of everything and you dare not separate them. If you do, you have reality falsely defined. If you have reality unfairly defined, it will not lead to enlightenment, it will not lead to truth. For Christians the Christ mystery of "Christ has died, Christ has risen, Christ will come again," is a mythic acclamation that describes that transformative movement from death to resurrection.

Fr. Richard Rohr

How should a mature Christian approach
Holy Week?

"We can't let Holy Week be just a kind of commemoration. It means contemplating the mystery of Jesus Christ as something which continues to work in our souls. The Christian is obliged to be alter Christus, ipse Christus: another Christ, Christ himself. Through baptism all of us have been made priests of our lives, 'to offer spiritual sacrifices acceptable to God through Jesus Christ.' Everything we do can be an expression of our obedience to God's will and so perpetuate the mission of the Godman."

Saint Josemaría Escrivá, 1902-1975

I ask myself: How do I plan on making Holy Week very different from every other week of the year?

Saturday of the Fifth Week of Lent

Transition to Holy Week

"From that time on, Jesus began to show his disciples that he must go to Jerusalem and suffer greatly from the elders, the chief priests, and the scribes, and be killed and on the third day be raised. Then Peter took him aside and began to rebuke him, "God forbid, Lord! No such thing shall ever happen to you." He turned and said to Peter, "Get behind me, Satan! You are an obstacle to me. You are thinking not as God does, but as human beings do." (Matthew 16: 21-23)

Tomorrow we begin Holy Week

On Palm Sunday the crowds welcomed **Jesus** to Jerusalem with loud *"Hosannas."* By Good Friday the same crowds were shouting, *"Crucify him! Crucify him!"*

What happened? Our salvation happened.

At every celebration of the Eucharist, we are spiritually brought back to the events of the evening of Holy Thursday, to the Last Supper and to what followed it on Holy Friday and Saturday.

Once again we see Jesus as he leaves the Upper Room, descends with his disciples to the Kidron valley and goes to the Garden of Olives. Even today that garden shelters some very ancient olive trees. Perhaps they witnessed what happened beneath their shade that evening, when Christ in prayer was filled with anguish, *"and his sweat became like drops of blood falling down upon the ground."* (Luke 22:44)

"The blood which shortly before Jesus had given to the Church as the drink of salvation in the sacrament of the Eucharist, began to be shed; its outpouring would then be completed on Golgotha to become the means of our redemption: *'Christ, as High Priest of the good things to come, entered once and for all into the Holy Place, taking not the blood of goats and calves but his own blood, thus securing an eternal redemption.'* (Heb 9:11-12)

"The Church was born of the Paschal Mystery. And yet the Pascal Mystery is different from the Eucharistic Mystery. On Holy Friday, no Eucharist is celebrated to make us realize that difference."

John Paul II,

Encycilical Ecclesia de Eucharistia, 2002

Now, not a prayer, but a task:
Decide how you will make Holy Week truly holy.

This concludes the Lenten Journey to Christian Maturity. However, Christian maturity is a day by day process. **Your local parish church will have a variety of Holy Week Services and suggestions to help you chart your course for this year's Holy Week. Enter into them as fully as you can. And may God Bless you in your journey to Christian maturity, which is, after all, a life long process.**

"For as Christ's sufferings overflow to us, so through Christ does our encouragement also overflow."

(2 Corinthians 1:5)

Author Biography

Father Bill Breslin was born in Red Bank, NJ shortly after the Second World War (1948). He is the fourth of four sons of Bertha and John Breslin. Bert was a school teacher and John was a salesman. He likes to think that he learned from his mother how to teach the faith, and from his father how to "sell" the faith. From his earliest days he wanted to become a priest and says that he must have gotten his vocation "in the womb." His home parish had a grammar school and a high school which he attended and then studied for the priesthood in Baltimore, Maryland. He was ordained in Red Bank in 1974 and learned how to be a priest in South Amboy, NJ. In 1977 he moved to Colorado to be closer to his family and served parishes in Denver, Northglenn, and Aurora and is presently in Boulder at Sacred Heart of Jesus. A hobby of his is blogging, so check out www.fatherbillsblog.com.

Other books by Pearn and Associates, Inc.

Walking in Snow, John Knoepfle

I Look Around for my Life, John Knoepfle

Ikaria, Anita Sullivan

The U Book, Nathan Preston Pierce

Another Chance, Joe Naiman

Goulash and Picking Pickles, Louise Hoffmann

Point Guard, Victor Pearn

Printed in the United States
134803LV00004B/6/P